EVERYBODY'S MOTHER

march 2003

To my amazing mum,
    Thank you for everything
but special thanks for teaching
me to be a mummy too.

Pen

Everybody's Mother

EDITED BY LINDA COGGIN & CLARE MARLOW

PETERLOO POETS

First published in 2001
by Peterloo Poets
The Old Chapel, Sand Lane, Calstock, Cornwall PL18 9QX, U.K.

**A catalogue record for this book is available
from the British Library**

ISBN   1 871471 94 X

Printed in Great Britain By
Antony Rowe Ltd, Chippenham, Wilts.

ACKNOWLEDGEMENTS

PETER ABBS: 'A Further Visit: February 1990' and 'A Girl in Sepia' from *Love After Sappho (Halfacrown Press 1999)*. Reprinted by kind permission of the publisher. FLEUR ADCOCK 'Willow Creek' and 'The Chiffonier' from *Poems 1960-2000 (Bloodaxe Books 2000)*. Reprinted by kind permission of the publisher. GILLLIAN ALLNUTT: Untitled – 'mother you never told me how to mend' and 'My mother the sea gives me' from *Beginning the Avocado (Virago 1987)* , reprinted by kind permission of the author. SIMON ARMITAGE: Untitled – 'Mother, any distance greater than a single span' from *Book of Matches (Faber and Faber 1992)*. Reprinted by kind permission of the publisher. MARGARET ATWOOD: 'Women Skating' from *Procedures Under Ground (Little Brown and Co & Oxford University Press)*. Reprinted by kind permission of the publisher. ELIZABETH BARTLETT: 'Contre Jour' from *Two Women Dancing (Bloodaxe)*. Reprinted by kind permission of the publisher. JEAN 'BINTA' BREEZE: 'For The Mother' from *Spring Cleaning (Virago Little Brown and Co)* Reprinted by kind permission of the publishers. CHRISTY BROWN: 'For My Mother' from *Come Softy To My Wake (Martin Secker and Warburg 1971)*. Reprinted by kind permission of The Random House Group Ltd. JIM BURNS: 'Aria' from *Confessions Of An Old Believer (Redbeck Press 1996)*. 'My Mother's Story' from *As Good A Reason As Any (Redbeck Press 1999)*. Reprinted by kind permission of the publishers. JOHN BURNSIDE: 'My Mother's Story' and 'Flitting' from *Feast Days (Martin Secker and Warburg)*. Reprinted by kind permission of The Random House Group Ltd. GILLIAN CLARKE: 'Her Table', 'The Habit of Light', 'Cut Glass', 'Elegy' and 'Shopping' from *Collected Poems (Carcanet Press Limited)*. Reprinted by kind permission of the publisher. COLIN FALCK: 'Mid August' from *Memorabilia (Stride Publications 1992)*. Reprinted by kind permission of the author. ELAINE FEINSTEIN: 'Calliope in the Labour Ward' from *Selected Poems (Carcanet Press Limited)*. Reprinted by kind permission of the publisher. U. A. FANTHORPE: 'Mother Scrubbing the Floor' from *Consequences (Peterloo Poets 2000)*. Reprinted by kind permission of the publisher. PETER FINCH: 'The Wisdom of Age' from *Food (Seren 2001)*. Reprinted by kind permission of the publisher. 'Rain' by kind permission of the author. LINDA FRANCE: 'How I learned the Names of Hedgerow Flowers' from *The Simultaneous Dress* 'My Mother, the Sea' from *Storyville (Bloodaxe Books 1997)*. Reprinted by kind permission of the publisher. JOHN FREEMAN: 'Surprise, Surprise' and 'One For Luck' from *Landscape with Portraits (Redbeck 1999)*. Reprinted by kind permission of the publisher. TONY HARRISON: 'Timer' and 'Isolation' from *Selected Poems (Penguin 1984)*. Reprinted by kind permission of the author. SEAMUS HEANEY: 'Mother' from *Door into the Dark (Faber and Faber 1969)*. Reprinted by kind permission of the publisher. JOHN HEGLEY: 'The brief Reunion' from *These were your Fathers (Methuen 1994)*. 'Living in a Mobile Home' from. *Glad To Wear Glasses (Andre Deutsch 1991)*. Reprinted by kind permission of PFD on behalf of John Hegley.

southwest arts

This collection is dedicated to
Jane, Barbara and Jean

Contents

Everybody's Mother

Of course,
everybody's mother always and
so on.............

Always never
loved you enough
or too smothering much.

Of course you were the Only One, your
mother
a machine
that shat out siblings, listen

everybody's mother
was the original frigid -
aire Icequeen clunking out
the hardstuff in nuggets, mirror-
silvers and ice-splinters that'd stick
in your heart.

Absolutely everyone's mother
was artistic when she was young.

Everyone's mother
was a perfumed presence with pearls, remote
white shoulders when she
bent over in her ball dress
to kiss you in your crib.

Everybody's mother slept with the butcher
For sausages to stuff you with.

Everyone's mother
mythologised herself. You got mixed up
between dragon's teeth and blackmarket stockings.

Naturally
she failed to give you
Positive Feelings
about your own sorry
sprouting body (it was a bloody shame)

but she did
sit up all night sewing sequins
on your carnival costume

so you would have a good time

and she spat
on the corner of her hanky and scraped
at your mouth with sour lace till you squirmed

so you would look smart.

And where
was your father all this time?
Away
at the war, or
in his office, or any-
way conspicuous for his
absence, so

what if your mother did
float around above you
big as a barrage balloon
blocking out the light?

Nobody's mother can't not never do nothing right.

Liz Lochhead

Untitled

Mother, any distance greater than a single span
requires a second pair of hands.
You come to help me measure windows, pelmets, doors,
the acres of the walls, the prairies of the floors.

You at the zero end, me with the spool of tape, recording
length, reporting metres, centimetres, back to base, then leaving
up the stairs, the line still feeding out, unreeling
years between us. Anchor. Kite.

I space-walk through the empty bedrooms, climb
the ladder to the loft, to breaking point, where something
has to give;
two floors below your fingertips still pinch
the last one-hundredth of an inch ....I reach
towards a hatch that opens on an endless sky
to fall or fly.

Simon Armitage

My Mother, the Sea

Let me tell you a secret about
my mother. She was a mermaid who wore
lipstick,bloody as sea anemones
underwater. She sat all day on a rock
combing her naturally auburn hair
and never had to go to work. She knew
where all the treasure chests lay buried
so she didn't give a whelk about money.

Because she was a mermaid she made
children in secret, with no pain; sent them
to school with the fishes, taught them how to
eat oysters in any month with a moon
to row them home. She was courted by Neptune
and Hollywood but much preferred knitting.
O her nets were the talk of the ocean!
Fine as spray and spindrift, flossed with fine pearls.

And I'm proud to be one of her daughters –
the way I swim so strong, length by length
the City Pool. My breaststroke's the envy
of dolphins. The scales of my skin match
her own. But now she's gone full fathom five
all I have left are her stories I knit
into patterns like wide blue waves I dive
into, never once coming up for air.

Linda France

My Mother the Diver

High cliffs, deep, deep water
dark blue green water swells
against the warm granite mass

a woman climbs down the steel boulders
between pink thrift, turfy grass and gulls
intent, careful, yet nimble and lithe

on the granite's edge she pauses,
naked and wrinkled and folded from many babies
she takes off her glasses and wearing only a swimming hat
she dives
down in to the jade depthsplash ripples – silence

she resurfaces, grinning from the shock of the cold
weightless body freed from its age
moving confidently in the rise and fall
of the salty Atlantic.

Lifted with the energy of the waves
the woman clings
to the rough rock, grazed knee
breathing hard and smiling
fearless and energetic.

Ellen Phethean

Willow Creek

The janitor came out of his eely cave
and said 'Your mother was a good swimmer.
Go back and tell her it's not yet time.'

Were there no other animals in Eden?
When she dives under the roots, I thought,
an eel is the last shape she'll want to meet.

Her brother was the only one for eels: farm-wise,
ruthless about food. You roll the skin back
and pull it off inside out like a stocking.

He grew up with dogs, horses and cattle.
She was more at home with water and music;
there were several lives for her after the creek.

In one of them she taught my younger son
to swim in the Greek sea; and walk through Athens
under a parasol, to buy us melon.

Fruit for the grandchildren, nectarines and pears
for the great-grandchildren; feijoa-parties........
'There's more of that to come', said the janitor.

'But no more swimming. Remember how she plunged
into a hotel pool in bra and knickers,
rather than miss the chance? She must have been sixty.'

I had some questions for the janitor,
But he submerged himself under the willows
In his cavern where I couldn't follow —

you have to be invited; I wasn't, yet,
and neither was she. Meanwhile, she's been allowed
a rounded segment of something warm and golden:

not pomegranate, paw-paw. She used to advise
eating the seeds: a few of them, with the fruit,
were good for you in some way – I forget.

Long life, perhaps. She knows about these things.
And she won't let a few eels bother her.
She's tougher than you might think, my mother.

Fleur Adcock

My mother the sea gives me

Alone inland where water wells
from a little mouth in the earth
a woman is beating her head on a stone.

None of the tales my mother handed down
to me hold her
heart's mountain.

She is a woman without an apron. Her truth
is forgotten.   Over and over
she drowns again in my bone-river.

Gillian Allnutt

Untitled

mother you never told me how to mend
the invisible hole   the soul
worn thin with wondering

all the world's a sheet
and the women in it   here to turn
sides to middle   when it gets torn   to begin
all over again with a stitch of thread

mother I cannot lie down in this bed   riddled with stitches
the pinned bones of the spine itch

it does not do and it does not do
to sit all day and sew

the light of another world filters through
these bare threads

the eye of the needle opens wide
to admit me

Gillian Allnutt

Parents' Day

I breathed shallow as I looked for her
in the crowd of oncoming parents, I strained
forward like a gazehound held back on a leash,
then I raced towards her. I remember her being
much bigger than I, her smile of the highest
wattage, a little stiff, sparkling
with consciousness of her prettiness – I
pitied the other girls for having mothers
who looked like mothers, who did not blush.
Sometimes she would have braids around her head like a
goddess or an advertisement for Californian raisins –
I worshipped her cleanliness, her transfixing
irises, sometimes I thought she could
sense a few genes of hers
dotted here and there in my body
like bits of undissolved sugar
in a recipe that did not quite work out.
For years, when I thought of her, I thought
of the long souring of her life, but on Parents' Day
my heart would bang and my lungs swell so I could
feel the tucks and puckers of embroidered
smocking on my chest press into my ribs,
my washboard front vibrate like scraped
tin to see that woman arriving
and to know that she was mine.

Sharon Olds

Mother o' Mine

If I were hanged on the highest hill,
Mother o' mine, O mother o' mine,
I know whose love would follow me still,
Mother o' mine, O mother o' mine.

If I were drowned in the deepest sea,
Mother o' mine, O mother o' mine,
I know whose tears would come down to me,
Mother o' mine, O mother o' mine.

If I were damned of body and soul,
Mother o' mine, O mother o' mine,
I know whose prayers would make me whole,
Mother o' mine, O mother o' mine.

Rudyard Kipling

Mother Scrubbing the Floor

She had a dancer's feet, elegant, witty.
We had our father's, maverick spreaders of dirt.

Dirt from London, dirt from Kent,
Mud, dust, grass, droppings, wetness, things,
Dirt, barefaced, dirt stinking, dirt invisible.

Whatever it was, she was ready:
The rubber kneeler, clanking galvanised bucket,
The Lifebuoy, the hard hot water.

Let me! We'd say, meaning. *Hate to see you do this
Too old. Too resentful. Besides, you'll blame us
That you had to do it.*

She never yielded. We couldn't do it right,
Lacking her hatred of filth, her fine strong hands.

Don't want you to do this, she said. *Don't want you to have to.
Just remember this: love isn't sex
But the dreary things you do for the people you love.
Home is the girl's prison,
The woman's workhouse,* she said.
Not me, she said. *Shaw.*
I do remember. I stand where she knelt.

U. A. Fanthorpe

Contre Jour

Contre jour, he said, a photographic phrase,
literally against the day, I suppose.
I'll put a little by, my mother would say,
against the day when we have nothing left.
Limp purse, well-rubbed, false teeth
not quite fitting, second-hand clothes,
knees like nutmeg graters. Whatever happened
to those gentle scented mothers sitting in gardens
under a shady hat, the maid mincing across the grass
with a tray for afternoon tea in early June?
it was never summer for her. It didn't reach
the dark back yard, the airless little rooms,
where the kitchen range brought a flush
to her face as she perpetually bent over it,
cooking, ironing, shifting sooty kettles round,
but never posed for her husband to catch
the tilt of her head against the day,
who never owned a camera anyway.

My inner lens clicks faster, faster,
contre jour, for now her face is fading
as her life recedes. You must have known
that once she minced across the lawn
carrying a loaded tray for mothers
like yours, whose photographs have
frames of silver, like the ones
she polished every week for twelve
pounds per annum and her keep.

Elizabeth Bartlett

21

Flitting

The feel of the maze
when I sleep in the afternoon
then wake a moment
in the house we left:
the furniture stacked in the van
and her going one last time
from room to room,
as if something had been
mislaid among the crates
and shrouded mirrors.
I hear us calling her still
till she comes to the door
in her raincoat and wine-coloured gloves,
like the girl in the school-book myth
who had known her way,
losing the thread at last, tired and surprised,
with nothing to keep her,
turning away from the silence.

John Burnside

Eternal Return

You happen again for a summer,
sit for a snapshot again on a broken wall,
a wave of shadow frozen in the grain
and poppies red again behind your smile.

That was a Thursday in August, in the speed
of youth, and it was Thursday when you died,
flexed against the rhythm of a cold
visitant; reduced to monochrome.

Now I am learning not to dream
in black and white,
watching the gold reappear in a run of shade,
and losing your absence. Learning to let it happen.

John Burnside

Ma

Old photographs would have her bookish, sitting
Under a willow. I take that to be a croquet
Lawn. She reads aloud, no doubt from Rupert Brooke.
The month is always May or June.

Or with the stranger on the motor-bike
Not my father, no. This one's all crew-cut
And polished brass buttons.
An American soldier, perhaps.
                              And the full moon
Swaying over Keenehan, the orchards and the cannery,
Thins to a last yellow-hammer, and goes.
The neighbours gather, all Keenehan and Colleglands.
There is storytelling. Old miners at Coalisland
Going into the ground. Singing, for fear of the gas,
The soft flame of a canary.

Paul Muldoon

A Girl in Sepia

Mother, there's still a bitterness on my tongue
And iron rusts near my heart. It's hell
To speak the truth. With you, I seldom did.
Absurdly shy, I was the kind of child who stared
And stuttered, to find long after the event the words
He hungered for. Tonght I look through photographs;
Here you are, a girl – in sepia – your First Communion:
All curls and frills. And here you are – in black and white –
Eighteen. Young. And vulnerable. And beautiful.
And here decades later – in Kodak colour –
The small, huddled, stubborn woman I remember.
I still wince before your flawed, excessive love;
Yet now, far too late, beyond the grave –
Ache to thank you – for the life you gave.

Peter Abbs

Mother, Dear Mother

She is invigilator; her name is knife.
She changes nappies and sleeps in my father's bed.

If I cry or trickle, she'll come to my whistle
And give me her breast. Or let me lie and cry.

Half of her's mine, and half is my hot fat father's.
To each, one arm, one eye – and then what?

What is the good of possessing half a woman?
I'll pull her down to me by her swinging hair

And eat her all up, moon-face, belly and toes,
And throw the skin to my father, to keep him warm.

Elma Mitchell

Surprise, Surprise

I only once visited my mother
without telling her I was coming.
I arrived late in the evening,
after a day with a friend.

Her face, when she opened the door,
was scrunched up in wrinkles,
lost in the dreariness of too
much solitary living.

She peered into the night blankly,
and then a light came on
in her face as she said my name,
as if I were longed-for relief.

Energy flowed through her
as if at the wave of a wand
I could have given and received
that happiness more often.

It was an afterthought
to a long-planned day
which I recall through mist,
an unalloyed happiness.

It shines from a colourless
landscape of many years,
like a bright light in a house
on the edge of a dark moor.

I could work out which year,
and from pettiness, may try:
but the moment needs no date,
present when I think of it.

I stayed two nights and took
the train back to my home.
They were perfectly happy days:
the moment prolonged and proved.

They too come back through the mist.
It is the moment that shines.
The turning point of surprise
strikes an undying spark.

John Freeman

One For Luck

My mother cuts down rowan trees,
puts shoes on the table, and she would,
if she had any reason to, walk under
any number of ladders, pass someone
on the stairs and set out round the world
on a Friday. She'll pour from the same
teapot as anyone, and magpies to her
are just birds, whether in pairs or not.
She's had a hard life and her feet
have tormented her during most of it,
but she's eighty-eight and in good health
apart from her feet, so would you say
she was lucky or unlucky? She spreads
old sandals and boots on the kitchen table,
looking for some she can adapt with glue,
bradawl and thread, and leather and Stanley knife.
No shoe-maker has ever understood,
though she's explained enough, and some
tried. The neighbours let their trees
grow wild, till her garden's a tunnel
in which nothing grows as it used to. I
lop some of the overhanging plum, watch
as she demolishes rowans on the other side.
The outside of the house needs painting. Men
will surround the house with their long ladders.
They won't get away with much. She'd be there,
making sure they strip the wood right down,
prime it and put two complete coats on, and
not leave any hardened drips of paint.
Then she'd walk back indoors with her stick,
threading her way under the ladders to make tea,
and bring it out to them with home-made buns.

John Freeman

You, Shiva, and My Mum

Shall I tell how she went to India
At the age of eighty
For a week in the monsoon

> Because her last unmarried son
> Was getting married to a girl
> With butter-yellow turmeric on her face

At the shrine of Maa Markoma
In the forest where Orissa's last
Recorded human sacrifice took place?

> How my mother rode a motorbike, pillion
> In the jungle at full moon
> Up a leopard-and leeches path,

Getting off to shove away
The sleeping buffalo,
Puddled shaves of sacred calf?

> How she who hates all frills
> Watched her feet painted scarlet henna,
> Flip-flop pattern between the toes

And backward swastikas at heel, without a murmur?
How she climbed barefoot to Shiva
Up a rock-side – where god sat

> Cross-legged, navy blue,
> On a boulder above his cave,
> One hand forbidding anyone

Impurely dressed in leather, to enter? How
She forded Cobra River
In a hundred degrees at noon

To reach the god's familiar – his little bull of stone,
A pinky blaze of ribbons, bells, hibiscus –
And, lifelong sceptic that she is,

The eyes of all
The valley on her – tribal, Hindu, atheist
And Christian – bowed? Would anyone

Believe me? Shall I tell how you
Laughed fondly at me for my pride
In her? How everything comes

Together because of you, and I can't say
Anything, whatever matters
(And what could matter more

Than that lit walk of hers uphill,
The things she'll do
And places she'll swan up in for

Her family), without your heart beside
My heart? How I wait on
The miracle

Of your breath in my ear?
Shall I tell
Them? Yes. Tell that.

Ruth Padel

The Third Light

The sexton is opening up the grave
Lining with mossy cushions and couch grass
This shaft of light, entrance to the earth
Where I kneel to marry you again,
My elbows in darkness as I explore
From my draughty attic your last bedroom.
Then I vanish into the roof space.

I have handed over to him your pain
And your preference for Cyprus sherry,
Your spry quotations from the *Daily Mail*
With its crossword solved in ink, your limp
And pills, your scatter of cigarette butts
And last-minute humorous spring-cleaning
Of one corner of a shelf in his cupboard.

You spent his medals like a currency,
Always refusing the third light, afraid
Of the snipers who would extinguish it.
Waiting to scramble hand in hand with him
Out of the shell hole, did you imagine
A Woodbine passing to and fro, a face
That stabilises like a smoke ring?

Michael Longley

The Balloon

You are a child in a dream and not my mother.
I float above your head as in a hot air balloon
That casts no shadow on you looking up at me
And smiling and waving and running without a limp
Across the shallow streams and fields of shiny grass
As though there were neither malformation nor pain.
This is the first time ever I have seen you running.
You are a child in the dream and not my mother
Which may be why I called out from the balloon to you:
'Jump over the hedges, Connie, jump over the trees.'

Michael Longley

Barrage Balloon

Bilious at being
too easily a mother,
you never surrendered
to the ceaseless noise and warfare of six siblings.
You rose over us, like a distant dirigible.

I remember pendulous breasts
and a bottom: two pillows
floating above me, rippling to my touch
in the green bathroom – songs your barrier
ignoring the whines of small charges.

I never quite pulled your attention down,
never intruded on the sacred two o'clock ceasefire
when you napped on the sofa, nappies at your feet,
an art book your pillow – Rembrandt or Renoir –
The Times your daily coverage.

Then your protective strategy was punctured,
over-ballasted by a seventh
you sunk lower, optimism gone.
With nothing to keep you airborne
you negotiated
a post-war reparation, tubes cut and sewn,
red scar forever across your belly,
making a limp balloon of your large presence.
You no longer bounced back to our demands.
It was difficult being an easy mother.

Ellen Phethean

The Chiffonier

You're glad I like the chiffonier. But I
feel suddenly uneasy, scenting why
you're pleased I like this pretty thing you've bought,
the twin of one that stood beside your cot
when you were small; you've marked it down for me;
it's not too heavy to be sent by sea
when the time comes, and it's got space inside
to pack some other things you've set aside,
things that are small enough to go by water
twelve thousand miles to me, your English daughter.
I know your habits – writing all our names
in books and on the backs of picture-frames,
allotting antique glass and porcelain dishes
to granddaughters according to their wishes,
promising me the tinted photograph
Of my great-grandmother. We used to laugh,
seeing how each occasional acquisition
was less for you than for later disposition:
'You know how Marilyn likes blue and white
china? I've seen some plates, I thought I might
 indulge in.' Bless you, Mother! But we're not
quite so inclined to laugh now that you've got
something that's new to you but not a part
of your estate: that weakness in your heart.
It makes my distance from you, when I go
back home next week, suddenly swell and grow
from thirty hours' flying to a vast
galactic space between present and past.
How many more times can I hope to come
to Wellington and find you still at home?
We've talked about it, as one has to, trying
to see the lighter aspects of your dying:
'You've got another twenty years or more'

I said, 'but when you think you're at death's door
Just let me know. I'll come and hang about
for however long it takes to see you out.'
'I don't think it'll be like that' you said:
'I'll pop off suddenly one night in bed.'
How secretive! How satisfying! You'll
sneak off, a kid running away from school —
well, that at least's the only way I find
I can bring myself to see it in my mind.
But now I see you in your Indian skirt
and casual cornflower-blue linen shirt
in the garden, under your feijoa tree,
looking about as old or young as me.
Dear little Mother! Naturally I'm glad
you found a piece of furniture that had
happy associations with your youth;
and yes, I do admire it — that's the truth:
its polished wood and touch of Art Nouveau
appeal to me. But surely you must know
I value this or any other treasure
of yours chiefly because it gives you pleasure.
I have to write this now, while you're still here:
I want my mother, not her chiffonier.

Fleur Adcock

Her Table

She fussed between kitchen and dining room
giving us all things to carry and do.
I see her two hand polishing a wine glass
until it gleams, immaculate.
She lifts it to the light and sets it down
on startched damask on the Christmas table.

On an ordinary Sunday it would be
a cut-glass jug of water, four tumblers.
As if these things could hold us, as if
they could make us flawless and ring true.

Gillian Clarke

The Habit of Light

In the early evening she liked to switch on the lamps
in corners, on low tables, to show off her brass,
her polished furniture, her silver and glass.
At dawn she'd draw all the curtains back for a glimpse
of the cloud-lit sea. Her oak floors flickered
in an opulence of beeswax and light.
In the kitchen, saucepans danced their lids, the kettle purred
on the Aga, supper on its breath and the buttery melt
of a pie, and beyond the swimming glass of old windows,
in the deep perspective of the garden, a blackbird singing,
she'd come through the bean rows in tottering shoes,
her pinny full of strawberries, a lettuce, bringing
the palest potatoes in a colander, her red hair bright
with her habit of colour, her habit of light.

Gillian Clarke

Shopping

Brought up with make do and mend, she wanted nice things.
Saturday shopping and afternoon tea at *The Angel*,
after haberdashery and household linen she'd move
in a trance through departments of china and glass
in the big city stores. As she moved, light sang
on the rims of tea-cups and glasses.
The shimmer stayed with her, reflecting her face
when she unpacked the parcels on the kitchen table
that stood on worn linoleum they couldn't afford to replace.

Gillian Clarke

Cut Glass

'She wanted you to have them,' he said.
'She knew you'd look after them.'
We polish them, her favourite cut glass,
making diamonds and rainbows.
She loved sparkle, parties, a ball-gown
with rhinestones, a touch of diamante.
She knew she was luminous
looking up from her sherry glass.
Even I felt my heart leap then.

Gillian Clarke

Elegy

'*Place but a kiss within the cup*,'
my father used to sing.
We drink from her glasses,
and I know you're thinking as we sip
that she touched them with her hands and lips.

Grief is diamond hard. It engraves the story on glass,
leaves nothing out. Sunlight swims on this page,
this table, in the tumbler of water like a shoal
of moving shallows, not quite shadows or smoke,
as the glass hardens and clears.

We fill our goblets with water,
cold pure risings from the deep
beneath our garden.
Each glass is archaeology
brimmed seepings
that have taken life-times to collect.

Into her crystal sherry glasses
pour us a *Fino*. Then a good wine
into fine Venetian crystal.
With this libation I remember her,
hold it to the light,
touch your glass with mine
on a pure note.

Gillian Clarke

Piano

SOFTLY, in the dusk, a woman is singing to me;
Taking me back down the vista of years, till I see
A child sitting under the piano, in the boom of the tingling
    strings
And pressing the small, poised feet of a mother who smiles
    as she sings.

In spit of myself, the insidious mastery song
Betrays me back, till the heart of me weeps to belong
To the old Sunday evenings at home, with winter outside
And hymns in the cosy parlour, the tinkling piano our
    guide.

So now it is vain for the singer to burst into clamour
With the great black piano appassionato. The glamour
Of childish days is upon me, my manhood is cast
Down in the flood of remembrance, I weep like a child for
    the past.

D.H. Lawrence

ERRATUM
Piano
First line of 2nd stanza should read:
In spite of myself, the insidious mastery of song

Getting to Go

When we'd done with Sunday school, she wasn't there.
Not then. Not soon. Not ever. No more Mum.
She had fallen on the landing by the stair,
Just coming up, and now she would never come.
Though I prayed and cried and prayed, God didn't care.

In The Edinburgh Infirmary she lay
On life support. We did not get to go,
And how she looked at last I cannot say.
They told us all they thought we ought to know.
My father went to see her every day,

Bess who had laughed and talked and smoked as late as
Twenty past two on Sunday afternoon,
Now emptied into absence, a hiatus
As uninhabitable as the Moon,
Something connected up to apparatus.

He watched the picture of Elizabeth
Jean Boyes, who was fat and witty, who was good
And kind and lost her temper, watched her breath
Pumped in, sucked out, her tubes, her bottled blood.
He watched the whole technology of death.

All this I think. Of course I do not know.
We did not see. We did not get to go.

John Whitworth

Going out with Mum

'Still got the umbrella dad gave me last Christmas.
Just fetch my gloves dear, no, the leather ones,
The ones I went to Baker Street to collect
And the man said "All change" and wouldn't let me stop
To think if I had everything.
Look in the other drawer. Have you seen my purse, John?
I know I had it. I'd just paid the milkman
And the phone rang. Look in the bathroom then.
Keys, money, letters. Have you got handkerchiefs?
Don't sniff, Bridget, blow. I must make sure
I've got the address right. D'you think you'd better take macs?
Just put the bread knife away dear, you never know
Who may get in and if they see one handy
It might – no, leave the kitchen window
There's the cat.'

We round the corner as the bus pulls off
From the bus stop. 'Now if you'd been ready
We might have caught that. It would have made all the difference.
There might not be another one for hours.'

We almost believe it's true it was our fault:
Mum's too good at being efficient for it to be hers.

Jenny Joseph

Have We Had Easter Yet?

"Who are you?" asks my mother.
"If you're looking after me
I ought to know your name."

I show her me when I was small,
A faded photograph.
"That's Bobbins," she says instantly.

"I wonder where she is, she never comes to see me."
I go away. To get my mother's lunch.
"How good it looks. Please thank the cook."

Later I find it in the bin.
"I didn't know who'd cooked it,
So I had those custard creams."

She smiles at me with faded, muddled eyes
And says my name,
Then struggles off on shaky legs,

Looks for her stick,
Opens the outside door,
Calls home dead dogs.

Alison Pryde

I Love me Mudder

I luv me mudder an me mudder luvs me
We cum so far from over the sea,
We heard that the streets were paved wid gold
Sometimes it's hot, sometimes it's cold,
I luv me mudder an me mudder luvs me
We try fe live in harmony
Yu might know her as Valerie
But to me she's just me mudder.

She shouts at me dad so loud sometime
She's always been a friend of mine
She's always doing de best she can
She works so hard down ina Englan,
She's always singin sum kinda song
She has big muscles an she very, very strong
She likes pussycats an she luvs cashew nuts
An she don't bother wid no ifs an buts.

I luv me mudder an me mudder luvs me
We cum so far from over de sea,
We heard that the streets were paved wid gold
Sometimes it's hot, sometimes it's cold,
I luv her and whatever we do
Dis is a luv I know is true,
My people, I'm talking to yu
Me an my mudder we luv yu too.

Benjamin Zephaniah

Beethoven's Mother

When the glazier
manoevres his rectangle of glass
across the street
like a slice of frozen lake,
I think of you;

when small flocks, roaming open fields
in autumn
like freed cyclamen,
on wings as thin as nasal blood-vessels
sing as they fly,
I think of you;

and when I read that Beethoven's mother,
cooking pastries
in the back streets of Cologne,
'lulls his overwrought feelings
into tranquillity',
of course I think I'm Beethoven with you.

Selima Hill

Chicken Feathers

1.
What a picture!
She has tucked her wild-looking chicken
under her arm and stares out
over what seems to be a mountain pass
on a windy day.
She is wearing a blue linen dress
the colour of summer.
She reminds me of Brunhilde – alone, bronzed, unfamiliar.
She doesn't look like anybody's mother.

2.
She used to love dancing.
She went to the Chelsea Ball
dressed as a leopard;
there she met my father,
who looked so dashing
in the Harlequin suit
his tailor made for him
from raw silk.
He had tiny shoes
like Cinderella's.
I have seen them.

3.
She comes to collect me from school,
on time, silent,
and I hand her my coat and satchel –
avoiding, even then, her lovely eyes,
that look down on my world
like distance stars.
I play with the girl next door,
and don't come home till bed-time.

4.
From the lighted window
I watch my mother
picking leeks in the twilight.

I will have soup
for my supper,
sprinkled with parsley.

She passes me my creamy bowl.
My hands are warm,
and smell of soap.

My mother's hands are cold as roots.
She shuts up the chickens
by moonlight.

5.
How can they think I an asleep
when he bends down and kisses
the nape of her neck,
and goes away to his own room,
while she sits in front of her mirror
and brushes and brushes
her waist-long silver hair?

6.
The hens are all gone.
How happy she used to be
setting out in her long tweed coat
across the orchard
with her bucket.
Chuck, chuck, chuck, she called
and they'd all come running.

7.
She walks behind the hedges
of the large garden, stooping
from time to time
to pick narcissi
for her mother's grave
now that it is Easter.
We don't want to go.
We're too young to remember
our grandmother –
and besides it will be cold
in the graveyard
where the wind blows
straight in off the downs.

8.
He went to his room with an orange
in his hand, and died there
sometime during the afternoon.
My mother spent the day in the kitchen.
When I came in from the garden
I was sent upstairs
to call him down to tea:
he was sitting by the window
with his back to me.
On the table beside him
were four boats made of orange peel,
with the pith piled neatly inside them.
My mother couldn't stand up.
She kept saying she was sorry,
but she couldn't stand up.
   It must be the shock she said.
It wasn't grief.
Come and sit down she said,
And have your tea.

9.
Tonight I kissed my mother,
for the first time that I can remember;
though I must have kissed her before,
as all daughters kiss their mothers.
She was passing in front of me
to kiss the children, and I leaned down
and touched her cheek with my lips.
It was easy – like the lighting of a candle.

10.
My sister always says
that on the morning out father died
he was working on the drawing of a liner
disappearing over a white horizon.
she says it is a symbol.
She's got the picture by her bed.
I would rather think of dying
as a coming into harbour,
a sort of final mooring.

11.
You put in at a little jetty.
There is someone there to welcome you –
not sinister – but rather surprising –
someone you know. In front of you rise
banks of fern and shinning celandines.
You can smell the woods.
They are full of life,
but very still.

12.
My mother and I, in our way,
understand each other.
when I kneel by her grave,
in need of a little consolation,
I will picture her standing
on a hillside in bright sunlight,
lifting her hand to wave to me;
or she is brushing away the feathers
that drift like dreams into her hair
and tickle her cheek, till she smiles?

Selima Hill

The Wisdom of Age

It's the end of the line in my
mother's beige living room. The
sun is across the floor in dancing
spikes. She's weeping under the faded
prints of two chrysanthemums. No tears
just the despair of age.
A fuse has tripped, she's clicked the
light switch until her fingers burn.
Nothing works. She's told me and god
and me again down her black, heavy
phone. Why is the world like
this? What have I done?
Now, together we must face the
faulty future – me standing there with
my yellow screwdriver and
my poultice of fuse-wire,
her with her poor hair
and her need which
clings to us both until we keel
wishing that wisdom would help
but knowing it can't.

Peter Finch

Rain

For my mother

How can I tell you about this? Me, always
full of what I am doing. I've been thirty years
trying to record how my pain can be ice rain
without knowing a thing about what pain really is.
Now, for you, the walls of the river are all that's left.
The rushing waters drive what was before them,
the past is worn to a veil of love and dust. Imagine this,
the mind giving it up, saying that's it, dissolving
as you watch, all of you swept away by the rush.
Time does this, the bastard clock, the drip that wears the
stone, the feet that shape the steps. Your old self
smiles at me through collapsing mud.

We walk in the garden where the plants no
longer have names and the birds are blurs.
You are holding onto me with that clutch of
yours that crushes bones. Who are we,
mother and son in a rain which keeps getting colder?
The mouth won't answer, it doesn't know,
but the body, that remembers.

Peter Finch

Aria

My mother always loved opera,
not that she ever got to see one,
and when a singer trilled high notes
from the old radio in our house,
she would pause and smile to herself.

I remember those moments.
The gloom of the small kitchen,
the smell of food cooking,
the hands wiped across the apron.
The peaceful look on her tired face.

Jim Burns

My Mother's Story

I visit my mother in hospital
and listen to what she has to say.
Is that cat still here, she asks,
and tells me to look under the bed.

It followed me in last night,
and won't go away. A small black cat,
not at all like Snowy,
the old white cat we once had.

Do you remember her? She used to wait
for my father to come home from the pit,
and she would run down the street,
and jump onto his shoulder.

He was a big man, over six feet tall,
and the neighbours, seeing Snowy
set against his grime, would shout
'There's Matt Wilson and his cat.'

Oh, she was a fine cat, Snowy was,
and he was a fine man, and didn't drink
like a lot of the miners did.
He dies in 1915, killed in France.

I thought you were coming yesterday?
No, I reply, I said today,
and she says, That's strange,
and why did I think it was yesterday?

Jim Burns

Sorting Through

The moment she died, my mother's dance dresses
turned from the colours they really were
to the colours I imagined them to be.
I can feel the weight of bumptoed silver shoes
swinging from their anklestraps as she swaggers
up the path towards *her* dad, light-headed
from airman's kisses. Here, at what I'll have to learn
to call *my father's house*, yes every
ragbag scrap of duster prints her even more vivid
than an Ilford snapshot on some seafront
in a white cardigan and that exact frock.
Old lipsticks. Liquid stockings.
Labels like Harella, Gor-Ray, Berketex.
As I manhandle whole outfits into bin-bags for Oxfam
every mote in my eye is a utility mark
and this is useful:
the sadness of dispossessed dresses,
the decency of good coats roundshouldered
in the darkness of wardrobes,
the gravitas of lapels,
the invisible danders of skin fizzing off from them
with all the life that will not neatly end.

Liz Lochhead

The Fitting Room

I was a legend in my mother's lifetime,
And marvelled as the name I never took
Did cute or comic things in simple rhyme,
And dazzled like an easy-reading book.
But I grew up, I said: *what happened after?*
My mother couldn't say. She'd have intoned:
'They are not long, the weeping and the laughter'
– Except she dared not entertain such .
And so she clung to starry dot-to-dots,
And at her side the child of fifty groaned.

I had no life to share, no word to say
Till she lay dying. Then the legend spoke,
Spoke legends in the colours she'd have chosen,
Perhaps, to light her steep descent from day.
Words failed her, though her mouth was twisted open
As if caught laughing at the little joke
Death makes of life. Since then, I've found a tongue
Too quick, I think, at argument and blame,
And yet I've half a hope she sits among
My readers – those who know my grown-up name.

She'll tell the tale that fits me like a glove,
And I won't feel diminished saying Mother,
Mummy, Mum. Why is so much of love
The kind of gift you know was made by hand,
And not made well – some weird, tenderly-knit
Garment that doesn't suit, won't ever fit?

I think it was her love I called a legend.
I thought it shrank me, sought an ampler space.
But she's the legend, now; the way I tell her,
My funny gift. My loss. My crooked face.

Carol Rumens (nee Carol-Ann)

Mother In Satin

On Saturday nights, my mother

took off her blue jeans,
put on a red satin dress
with a wide circle skirt
that swished when she danced.

Or, a black brocade sheath dress
with a peplum of white lace
and rhinestone earrings
that jangled like ice-cubes.

Or, to backyard parties, a pink
waffle pique with a sewn-in
brassiere and laces up the back.

In Springalator high heels
open at the toe, she twirled
across the patio onto the grass,

unwinding like a bolt of organza,
her *Tabu* perfume simmering
in the torchlight, she danced
past the clothesline, past the built-in
barbecue, past the ornamental
fish pond, turning
into herself for the night.

Donna Hilbert

In the Attic

Even though we know now
your clothes will never
be needed, we keep them
upstairs in a locked trunk.

Sometimes I kneel there
touching them, trying to relive
time you wore them, to catch
the actual shape of arm and wrist.

My hands push down
between hollow, invisible sleeves,
hesitate, then take hold
and lift:

a green holiday; a red christening;
all your unfinished lives
fading through dark summers
entering my head as dust.

Andrew Motion

At the Dressing Table Mirror

She sits at the dressing table, pushing back her hair,
Lipstick in hand, eyes poised above the quivering stick,

Aware of someone – a boy moving behind her, watching,
Observing the dark hair falling onto her shoulders

And trying to remove without her noticing
A thing she cannot see from the handbag on the bed:

But she has only to turn to her right to check on his movements
And the reflection that showed her now shows the boy also

And what he does beside her in that mirror, in the room
They both occupy ....United for an instant

In that glance, surprised by the net in which they find
Themselves doing what their image shows them doing.

They break on the very edge of laughter, clearer for
A second in that marriage, till she leans forward to

Apply the lipstick, when her breathing mists the glass
And the boy and the woman are parted. But still, many years after

Throwing out old books, or turning up a card
In her writing, or noticing a look in his daughter's eye

To arrest him at his work, he sees at once the mirror
And hears again their shared and broken laughter.

George Szirtes

The Armada

Long long ago
when everything I was told was believable
and the little I knew was less limited than now,
I stretched belly down on the grass beside a pond
and to the far bank launched a child's armada.
A broken fortress of twigs,
the paper-tissue sails of galleons,
the waterlogged branches of submarines –
all came to ruin and were on flame
in that dusk-red pond.
And you, mother, stood beside me,
impatient to be going,
old at twenty-three, alone,
thin overcoat flapping.
How closely the past shadows us.
In a hospital a mile or so from that pond
I kneel beside your bed and, closing my eyes,
reach out across forty years to touch once more
that pond's cool surface,
and it is your cool skin I'm touching;
For as on a pond a child's paper boat
was blown out of reach
by the smallest gust of wind,
so too have you been blown out of reach
by the smallest whisper of death,
and a childhood memory is sharpened,
and the heart burns as the armada burnt,
long, long ago.

Brian Patten

Isolation

I cried once as a boy when I'd to leave her
at Christmas in the fourth year of the War,
taken to Killingbeck with scarlet fever,
but don't cry now, although I see once more
from the window of the York-Leeds diesel back
for her funeral, my place of quarantine,

and don't, though I notice by the same railtrack
hawthorns laden with red berries as they'd been
when we'd seen them the day that we returned
from the hospital on this same train together
and she taught me a country saying that she'd learned
as a child: *Berries bode bad winter weather!*

and don't, though the fresh grave's flecked with sleet,
and dad, with every fire back home switched on, 's
frozen,
      and don't,
               until I hear a bleat
round the ransacked house for his long johns.

Tony Harrison

Timer

Gold survives the fire that's hot enough
to make your ashes in a standard urn.
An envelope of coarse official buff
contains your wedding ring which wouldn't burn.

Dad told me I'd to tell them at St James's
that the ring should go in the incinerator.
that 'eternity' inscribed with both their names is
His surety that the'd be together 'later'.

I signed for the parcelled clothing as the son,
the cardy, apron, pants, bra, dress –
the clerk phoned down: 6 - 8 - 8 – 3 - 1?
Has she still her ring on? (Slight pause.) *Yes!*

It's on my warm palm now, your burnished ring!
I feel your ashes, head, arms, breasts, womb, legs,
sift through its circle slowly, like that thing
you used to let me watch to time the eggs.

Tony Harrison

Women Skating

A lake sunken among
cedar and black spruce hills;
late afternoon.

On the ice a woman skating,
jacket sudden
red against the white,

concentrating on moving
in perfect circles.

(actually she is my mother, she is
over at the outdoor skating rink
near the cemetery. On three sides
of her there are streets of brown
brick houses; cars go by; on the
fourth side is the park building.
The snow banked around the rink
is grey with soot. She never skates
here. She's wearing a sweater and
faded maroon earmuffs, she has
taken off her gloves).

Now near the horizon
the enlarged pink sun swings down.
Soon it will be zero.

With arms wide the skater
turns, leaving her breath like a diver's
trail of bubbles.

Seeing the ice
as what it is, water:
seeing the months
As they are, the years
in sequence, occuring
underfoot, watching
the miniature human
figure balanced on steel
needles (those compasses
floated in saucers) on time
sustained, above
Time circling: miracle

Over all I place
a glass bell.

Margaret Atwood

Keeping Orchids

The orchids my mother gave me when we first met
are still alive, twelve days later. Although

some of the buds remain closed as secrets.
Twice since I carried them back, like a baby in a shawl,

from her train station to mine, then home. Twice
since then the whole glass carafe has crashed

falling over, unprovoked, soaking my chest of drawers.
All the broken waters.. I have rearranged

the upset orchids with troubled hands. Even after
that the closed ones did not open out. The skin

shut like an eye in the dark; the closed lid.
Twelve days later, my mother's hands are all I have.

Her face is fading fast. Even her voice rushes
through a tunnel the other way from home.

I close my eyes and try to remember exactly:
a paisley pattern scarf, a brooch, a navy coat.

A digital watch her daughter was wearing when she died.
Now they hang their heads,

and suddenly grow old – the proof of meeting. Still,
her hands, awkward and hard to hold

fold and unfold a green carrier bag as she tells
the story of her life. Compresed. Airtight.

A sad square, then a crumpled shape. A bag of tricks.
Her secret life – a hidden album, a box of love letters.

A door opens and closes. Time is outside waiting.
I catch the draught in my winter room.

Airlocks keep the cold air out.
Boiling water makes flowers live longer.

So does cutting the stems with a sharp knife.

Jackie Kay

My Mother Said

Barnes, Buntysweet,
Bonks and A-Becket,
Naming her brood
Like a farmer's wife.
Momo, wetty, winkle-words
Safe as blancmange
Bosoms in opaque nighties.
Maresey doats and
The blush fucket
Don't step in the dogsh.
Reaching for blankets
Words surface,
Spoonerish and nursey rude,
Out of my mouth, her rubbish talk
That smooths, soothes
Difficult little lives.

Ellen Phethean

Living in a Mobile Home

my mum lives in a mobile home
it may sound odd to some
but does it to my mum?
no – it doesn't to my mum
it may be small but she's not very tall
and she's got all she needs
heating
lighting
hot water
a roof
To tell you the truth when you're inside
it's hard to believe that you're living in a mobile home
she wants to keep her mobile home as long as she can
she doesn't want a mansion or a caravan
a mobile home is just the place for my Mummy
Mention a mobile home
and she puts up her thumby
but there's always room for home improvements
even in an ideal home
and whenever there's a windy day
I hope my mother's mobile home won't blow away
because if it did I don't know what my mum would say
but anyway
there's sliding doors
there's wall to wall floors
and there's plenty of room
so you can have a party

you can let yourself go
you can show a home movie
you can have a game of cricket
with your telly as a wicket
and you can do the bosanova
without knocking your dog over

John Hegley

After the Last Breath
(JH 1813-1904)

There's no more to be done, or feared, or hoped;

None need now watch, speak low, and list, and tire;
No irksome crease outsmoothed, no pillow sloped
Does she require.

Blankly we gaze. We are free to go or stay;
Our morrow's anxious plans have missed their aim;
Whether we leave tonight or wait till day
Counts as the same.

The lettered vessels of medicaments
Seem asking wherefore we have set them here;
Each palliative its silly face presents
As useless gear.

And yet we feel that something savours well;
We note a dumb relief witheld before;
Our well-beloved is prisoner in the cell
Of Time no more.

We see by littles now the deft achievement
Whereby she has escaped the Wrongers all;
In view of which our momentary bereavement
Outshapes but small.

Thomas Hardy 1904
(JH is Jemima Hardy, the poet's mother)

How I Learned the Names of Hedgerow Flowers

My mother, Lily, lonely and beautiful flower,
poured out swathes with every cup
of tea from the thick brown pot:

celandine, dog rose, orchis, dock.

Each new packet, fragrant with the promise
of a fresh species, sweet dry leaves,
bloomed another, roughly daubed:

hawthorn, gorse, harebell, vetch.

I stuck the right ones in their white spaces,
gathering posies, the smell of summer,
singing the chain of their names in my head:

speedwell, ragwort, eyebright, broom.

Later, when the album was lost
and all I collected were cracked pavements,
flowers ran wild in my heart:

foxglove, teasel, cowslip, thrift.

Linda France

The Brief Reunion   (La Reunion Breve)

In spite of all the beatings
and the bile
the thing I most remember about my father
Is the smile he wore
the time he saw
his Parisian mother for the first time
in seventeen years
and I heard him talking his first language
for the first time in my life
and the tears flowed down their faces
as they nattered on like nut-cases.
She was a poor and very ancient woman
but somehow she'd got the money together
to come over and see her similarly unwealthy son.

The following morning after my dad had gone to work
my grandmother interrupted my mother's household duties
with the suggestion of an unscheduled coffee break.
when my dad came back that evening
and enquired as to the whereabouts of our visitor
my mum explained that she had had to go home early
because she was an old cow.

John Hegley

The Waiting Lists

The first agency we went to
didn't want us on their lists,
we didn't live close enough to a church
nor were we church-goers
(though we kept quiet about being Communists).
The second told us
we weren't high enough earners.
The third liked us
but they had a five-year waiting list.
I spent six months trying not to look
at swings nor the front of supermarket trolleys,
not to think this kid I've wanted could be five.
The fourth agency was full up.
The fifth said yes but again no babies.
Just as we were going out the door
I said oh you know we don't mind the colour.
Just like that, the waiting was over.

This morning a slim manilla envelope arrives
postmarked Edinburgh: one piece of paper
I have now been able to look up your microfiche
(as this is all the records kept nowadays).
From your mother's letters, the following information:
Your mother was nineteen when she had you.
You weighed eight pounds four ounces.
She liked hockey. She worked in Aberdeen
as a waitress. She was five foot eight inches.

I thought I'd hid everything
that there wasnie wan
giveaway sign left

I put Marx Engels Lenin(no Trotsky)
in the airing cupboard — she'll no be
checking out the towels surely

All the copies of the **Daily Worker**
I shoved under the sofa
the dove of peace I took down from the loo

A poster of Paul Robeson
saying give him his passport
I took down from the kitchen
I left a bust of Burns
my detective stories
and the Complete Works of Shelley

She comes as 11.30 exactly
I pour her coffee
from my new Hungarian set

And foolishly pray she willnae
ask its origins — honestly
this baby is going to my head

She crosses her legs on the sofa
I fancy I heard the **Daily Workers**
rustle underneath her

Well she says, you have an interesting home
She sees mu eyebrows rise.
It's different she qualifies.

Hell and I've spent all morning
trying to look ordinary
— a lovely home for the baby.

She buttons her coat all smiles
I'm thinking
I'm on the home run

But just as we get to the last post
her eye catches at the same time as mine
a red ribbon with twenty world peace badges

Clear as a hammer and sickle
on the wall,
Oh, she says are you against nuclear weapons?

To Hell with this. Baby or no baby.
Yes I says. Yes yes yes.
I'd like this baby to live in a nuclear free world.

Oh. Her eyes light up
I'm all for peace myself she says,
and sits down for another cup of coffee.

Jackie Kay

From Stranraer, South

Looking back, I can say, with my hand on my heart
that my mother got sick the day I said I was in love
with a girl who lived round the corner –
and never got better.

So Aileen McCleod left the day after my mother collapsed.
She caught the afternoon train from Stranraer, south.
My mother wouldn't open her mouth –
and never got better.

Friends brought me news of Aileen, here, there,
and she herself sent me two letters.
The first said come now; the second don't bother; yet my mother
never did get better.

I don't know if it's me or if it's her, but I'm sure
a certain expression of satisfaction crosses her cheeks
when I give her a bed bath, as if she's taught me a lesson
it will never get better.

I see myself in our hall mirror smiling at my mother's smile,
complicit, apologetic, I know what you're up to.
No matter what I do I can't wipe that look from my face.
It will never get better.

I carry in holy water. I lift her head. Tilt her chin.
I dab round her smile with soft flannelette.
I bring the commode and stroke her hand. Fresh sheets.
It will never get better,

better than this, for what is a life for but to be a good daughter
and love your mother's weakness and moisten her lips
and listen to the sound of her dreams in waves
and see the stars outside flicker and waver, uncertain.

Jackie Kay

My Mother on a Seat Outside a Hospital

Too early for the bus, my mother
and her sister have walked a dozen dark-
to-daylight miles through a wood, by quiet roads,
to sit on a bench beside a flower bed,
colours that release their scent
in the evening, and to wait while her husband
dies on a ward already awake
that she might have visited after all.

He was the man before my father,
young, clean-shaven, just moved where work was.
If he'd not loved swimming so much
or had known that pool, which end was which,
or if he'd shallow-dived, I'd not exist;
and Mum too would be a different person,
spared the tragedy she mentioned
the other night in passing, a young wife
with two babies – my big sisters – and with my brother
forming inside her, who must manage
from that moment as best they can alone
in a strange town between the wars.

But there she is, just as she is, and so I can see
through that depth of water the spine
snapping, and the man who was not my father
bobbing to the air ...It took him days to die
where, outside on a municipal bench,
two young women, girls they called themselves,

are anxious and not tired,
deciding to give it another half-hour –
despite the sixth sense that sent them there
before bothering anyone so early.

Peter Sansom

Distances

When she falls backwards and meets the fire and the rain,
Last of her generation in this absurdly continent family,
Who will remember her, make a note of her overwhelming virtues,
And colourful evasions: who will truthfully describe
The face that always remained a stubborn child's,
Outstaring us with hardiness, impudence, fear:
Who will follow that stare to the father:
Who will stand at the grave and tell him she was hurt:
Who will show the mother and sister what they stole:
Who will ask the young man, disappointed and disappointing,
For one of those Valentine poems she smiled at and soon mislaid
(the ever-blue handwriting knotted with shyest self-declaration):
Who'll untangle the whiteness and free all the numerous shapes
            of her lips?

They will say, those greatest of aunts, those most-removed cousins
Whose names she almost remembered, that it's not up to them
Since she leaves a child: this is the child's business.

Don't look at me. I'm innocent. I'm not the one
To speak of the dead. I can't even speak to the living.

Carol Rumens

Dead March

It's twenty years (*It's not, it's twenty three—*
be accurate) since you were whisked away
(*I wasn't 'whisked away'; I broke my skull*)
and I was left to contemplate your life,
(*My life? Ridiculous. You mean my death.*)

Well, twenty/twenty-three. I can't decide
if that's a long time or no time at all,
or whether everything I've said since then,
and thought, and done, to try and work out how
the way we treat our lives might be involved
with how our lives treat us is more than just
a waste of breath. That's right. A waste of breath.

You see, you're always with me even though
you're nowhere, nothing, dead to all the world —
you interrupt me when I start to talk,
you are the shadow, dragging at my heels.
This means I can't step far enough away
to get the thing I want you to explain
in focus, and I can't lean close enough
to hear the words you speak and feel their weight.

And if I could, what difference would it make?
It's like I said, I can't decide, it's just
that having you suspended all these years
at some clear mid-point between life and death
has made me think you might have felt your way
along the link between the two, and learnt
how one deserves the other. Or does not.

I feel I'm standing on a frozen pond
entranced by someone else below the ice,
a someone who has found out how to breathe
the water, and endure the cold and dark.
I know I ought to turn my back. I can't.

I also know that if I just stay put
and watch the wax-white fingers flop about
I'll start to think they must be beckoning.
I'll stare and stare and stare and stare and stare.
It's twenty years since you were whisked away,
or twenty-three. That's more than half my life.

Andrew Motion

Mid-August

Mid-August. The summer holding unnaturally,
The heat full-on. The unchanging view
From the hospital window
And still no rain.

                    It was the kind of summer

You wanted life to be.
Your dying
Is what we shall remember it by.

And now you are at rest in this overgrown
Cemetery corner, buried with your only husband
By your only son.
The bees rummage the landscape for what's left in it.
Your gentleness gone
We are all a shade nearer barbarity.

The city macerates its lusts.
Girls at the bus-stops proffer their thighs
To the future.
Something will come of it.

I have a picture of you
In a shaded college garden walk,
Alone and unprotected (I was behind the camera),
A little lost; imagining perhaps
Some restoring triumph for me

—A setting to rights —
You would never live to see me realise.

I will do what I can.

Colin Falck

A Further Visit: February 1990

For my mother

Back – and at each glance the town contracts.
How dwarf the buildings seem that once towered
Over me. All close-ups then; and sticky palms.
We take the bitter route along the promenade.
You talk of latest deaths, lives slowly
Extinguished, last words said. At each return
There are further casualties to add. The sea
Is out; the iron defences bleed an oxide red.
At the cemetery we clear the grave. You plant
A rose. I touch the stone, sense Father's back:
White. Emaciated. Cold. A frenzied wind
Tears at our throats. The driven clouds blacken
The sun. I kiss you from the moving train.
The scene blurs behind me. It begins to rain.

Peter Abbs

For My Mother

Only in your dying, Lady, could I offer you a poem.

So uncommonly quiet you lay in our grieving midst
        your flock of bereaved wild geese
pinioned by the pomp and paraphernalia of death
        for once upon a rare time wordless
beyond the raw useless grief of your nine fine sons
        the quiet weeping of your four mantillaed daughters
gathered in desperate amity around your calm requiem hour
        and almost I saw you smile in happy disbelief
from the better side of the grave.

Only in your dying, Lady, could I offer you a poem.

Never in life could I capture that free live spirit of girl
        in the torn and tattered net of my words.
Your life was a bruised flower
        burning on an ash-heap
strong and sure on the debris of your broken decades
        unwilting under a hail of mind-twisted fate
under the blind-fisted blows of enraged love
        turning ever toward the sun of a tomorrow
you alone perceived beyond present pain.

Only in your dying, Lady, could I offer you a poem.

You were a song inside my skin
        a sudden sunburst of defiant laughter
spilling over the night-gloom of my half awakenings
        a firefly of far splendid light
dancing in the dim catacombs of my brain.
        Light of foot and quick of eye for pain
you printed patterns of much joy upon the bare walls of my life
        with broad bold strokes of your Irish wit
flaming from the ruins of your towers.

Only in your dying, Lady, could I offer you a poem.

With gay uplifted finger you beckoned
      and faltering I followed you down paths
I would not otherwise have known or dared
      limping after you up that secret mountain
where you sang without need of voice or words.
      I touched briefly the torch you held out
and bled pricked by a thorn from the black deep rose of your
                                 courage.
      From the gutter of my defeated dreams
you pulled me to heights almost own.

      Only in your dying, Lady, could I offer you a poem.

I do not grieve for you
      in your little square plot of indiscriminate clay
for now shall you truly dance.

O great heart
    O best of all my songs
      the dust be merciful upon your holy bones

Christy Brown

Untitled

My mother's stitchery
by oil-light, bright needle
pricking linen with petals
taut as tambourine
beneath tight black eyes

Come quick, my father calls
come do something useful.
She anchors the skein
who never did anything
not useful, but this

They kneel down together
in the sty by oil-light
the feverish sow between them
a small sister, brown hands
travelling her white lard

Your mother was beautiful
father tells me one day.
it is a strange saying.
his eyes that have known more
than mine seem to say less

That fine work by oil-light
he tells her, wrinkles your eyes
but occasions for it
don't stop, nor she, save to suck
new silk for the needle's eye

All her care is dispersed
now, given or gone away
under some several roofs
my sisters and I
all her useless stitchery.

Paul Hyland

Family Affairs

No longer here the blaze that we'd engendered
Out of pure wrath. We pick at quarrels now
As fussy women stitch at cotton, slow
Now to forget and too far to surrender,
The anger stops, apologies also.

And in this end of summer, weighted calm
(Climate of mind, I mean), we are apart
Further than ever when we wished most harm.
Indifference lays a cold hand on the heart;
We need the violence to keep us warm.

Have we then learnt at last how to untie
The bonds of birth, umbilical long cord,
So that we live quite unconnected by
The blood we share? What monstrous kind of sword
Can sever veins and still we do not die?

Elizabeth Jennings

Calliope in the Labour Ward

she who has no love for women
married and housekeeping

now the bird notes begin
in the blood in the June morning
look how these ladies are
as little squeamish as
men in a great war

have come into their bodies
as their bran dwindles to
the silver circle on
eyelids under sun
and time opens
pain in the shallows to wave up and over them

grunting in gas and air
they sail to a
darkness without self
where no will reaches

in that abandon less
than human
give birth
bleak as a goddess

Elaine Feinstein

Mother

As I work at the pump, the wind heavy
With spits of rain is fraying
The rope of water I'm pumping.
It pays itself out like air's afterbirth
At each gulp of the plunger.

I am tired of the feeding of stock.
Each evening I labour this handle
Half an hour at a time, the cows
Guzzling at bowls in the byre.
Before I have topped up the level
They lower it down.

They've trailed in again by the readymade gate
He stuck into the fence: a jingling bedhead
Wired up between posts. It's on its last legs.
It does not jingle for joy any more.

I am tired of walking about with this plunger
Inside me. God, he plays like a young calf
Gone wild on a rope.
Lying or standing won't settle these capers,
This gulp in my well.

O when I am a gate for myself
Let such wind fray my waters
As scarfs my skirt through my thighs,
Stuffs air down my throat.

Seamus Heaney

Maternity

One wept whose only child was dead,

New-born, ten years ago.

'Weep not; he is in bliss,' they said.

She answered, 'Even so,

Ten years ago was born in pain

A child, not now folorn,

But oh, ten years ago, in vain,

A mother, a mother was born.'

Alice Meynell

Post-natal

Being a midwife, you were different
to other mothers, never fussed. You fed
and calmly cared for three generations
under the same roof.

My father once said he was heart-broken
when you left me in my cot, closed the door,
and told him I'd stop crying once I knew
you wouldn't come.

Lately, like a child, I've woken crying,
hungry to see you, touch you, talk to you.
I think you hear me in some far-off room,
would come now if you could.

We all have a second umbilical cord –
the one we never see, that is our making.
It feeds comfort from wherever you are now;
do not cut it.

Marion Lomax

For The Mother

she

blazed

comet trails

from the oil

of her burning lamps

through the lonely vigil

of the night

dispelling

clouds of doom

she opened

trajectories

of sky

woven in her womb

she

rolled

away the stone

blocking an empty tomb

to prove

we are not here

we

are

risen

Jean 'Binta' Breeze

Strength and dignity are her clothing;

And she laugheth at the time to come.

She openeth her mouth to wisdom;

And the law of kindness is her tongue.

She looketh well to the ways of her household,

And eateth not the bread of idleness;

Her children rise up and call her blessed,

Her husband, also, and he praiseth her, saying:

'Many daughters have done virtuously

But thou excelleth them all.'

NOTES ON THE EDITORS

Linda Coggin performed in theatre and the alternative cabaret circuit before presenting a series of programmes for Thames T.V. Now a mother, she writes and performs poetry.

Clare Marlow had a career as a primary teacher and then a lecturer. Now retired, she does what she likes. She is a daughter, a sister, a mother and a granny.

ACKNOWLEDGEMENTS (CONTINUED)

DONNA HILBERT: 'Mother in Satin' from *Deep Red* (*Desert Hot Springs 1993*). Reprinted by kind permission of the author. SELIMA HILL: 'Beethoven's Mother' from *Trembling Hearts in the Bodies of Dogs* (*Bloodaxe Books*). Reprinted by kind permission of the publisher. 'Chicken Feathers' reprinted by kind permission of the author. PAUL HYLAND: Untitled 'My mother's stitchery' from *Poems of Z* (*Bloodaxe Books*). Reprinted by kind permission David Higham Associates. ELIZABETH JENNINGS: 'Family Affairs' from *Collected Poems* (*Carcanet*). Reprinted by kind permission David Higham Associates. JENNY JOSEPH 'Going out with Mum' from *All The Things I See* (*Macmillan Children's Books 2000*). Reprinted by kind permission of the author. JACKIE KAY: 'The Waiting Lists' from *The Addoption Papers* (*Bloodaxe Books, 1991*). 'From Stranraer South' from *Off Colour* (*Bloodaxe Books, 1998*). 'Keeping Orchards' from *Other Lovers* (*Bloodaxe Books 1993*). Reprinted by kind permission of the publisher. RUDYARD KIPLING: 'Mother O' Mine' from *Rudyard Kipling's Verses: The Definitive Edition* (*Hodder & Stoughton, 1912*). Reprinted by kind permission of A.P. Watt Ltd. on behalf of The National Trust for Places of Historic Interest or Natural Beauty. D. H. LAWRENCE: 'Piano' from *The Complete Poems of D.H. Lawrence*. Reprinted by kind permission of Laurence Pollinger Limited and the Estate of Frieda Laurence Ravagli. LIZ LOCHHEAD: 'Everbody's Mother' from *Dreaming Frankenstein & Collected Poems* (*Polygon 1984*). Copyright © Liz Lochhead. 'Sorting Through' from *Penguin Modern Poets 4*. Reprinted by kind permission of the author and the publishers. MARION LOMAX: 'Post-natal' from *Raiding The Borders* (*Bloodaxe Books 1996*). Reprinted by kind permission of the publisher. MICHAEL LONGLEY: 'The Third Light' from *Poems 1963-1983* and 'The Balloon' from *Gorse Fires*. Reprinted by kind permission of the author. ELMA MITCHELL: 'Mother Dear Mother' from *The Human Cage* (*Peterloo Poets, 1979*). Reprinted by kind permission of the publisher. ANDREW MOTION: 'Dead March' and 'In The Attic' from *Selected Poems* (*Faber & Faber*). Reprinted by kind permission of the publisher. PAUL MULDOON: 'Ma' from *Mules* (*Faber and Faber*). Reprinted by kind permission of the publisher. SHARON OLDS: 'Parents Day' from *The Wellspring*. Copyright © 1996 by Sharon Olds. Reprinted by kind permission of Alfred A. Knopf, a division of Random House, Inc. RUTH PADEL: 'You, Shiva and My Mum' by kind permission of the author. BRIAN PATTEN: 'The Armada' from *Armada*. Reprinted by kind permission of HarperCollins Ltd. ELLEN PHETHEAN: 'My Mother Said' from *Sauce* (*Bloodaxe Books 1994*). 'My Mother the Diver' and 'Barrage Balloon', printed by kind permission of the author. ALISON PRYDE: 'Have We Had Easter Yet?' from *Have We Had Easter Yet?* (*Peterloo Poets 1998*). Reprinted by kind permission of the publisher. CAROL RUMENS: 'The Fitting Room' from *Thunberscrew No 7* (*Edited by Tim Kendal, 1997*). *Reprinted by kind permission of the author*. 'Distances' from *Best China Sky* (*Bloodaxe Books, 1995*). Reprinted by kind permission of the publisher. PETER SANSOM: 'My Mother on a Seat Outside a Hospital' from *Point Of Sale* (*Carcanet Press Ltd*). Reprinted by kind permission of the publisher. GEORGE SZIRTES: 'At the Dressing Table Mirror' from *The Budapest File* (*Bloodaxe Books 2000*). Reprinted by kind permission of the publisher. JOHN WHITWORTH: 'Getting to Go' from *Landscape with Small Humans* (*Peterloo Poets 1993*). Reprinted by kind permission of the publisher. BENJAMIN ZEPHANIAH: 'I Luv me Mudder' from *Wicked World* (*Puffin Books 2000*). Reprinted by kind permission of the author.

While effort has been made to contact copyright holders, sometimes this has not been possible. The publisher will be pleased to hear from any copyright holder not here acknowledged and to rectify any apparent infringement at the earliest possible opportunity.